# AUSTRALIA
# IN PICTURES

# AUSTRALIA IN PICTURES

## GEOFF HIGGINS

Page 1: The Flinders Ranges, South Australia.

Pages 2-3: View of the Whitsunday Passage from Shute Harbour.

Pages 4-5: Sunset over Darling Harbour.

Pages 6-7: London Bridge, an unusual formation near Port Campbell, Victoria.

Pages 8-9: Russell Falls, Mount Field National Park, Tasmania.

Pages 10-11: Sunset, the Flinders Ranges, South Australia.

Pages 12-13: Quobba Point, near Carnarvon, Western Australia.

Pages 14-15: Landscape near Maryvale, southwest of Alice Springs.

Page 17: Sturt's Desert Pea.

Page 16: A wallaby with a 'joey' in her pouch.

Title page: Pelicans

Front cover: 'The Three Sisters' at Katoomba in the Blue Mountains.

Left: Rich silver-lead deposits have made Mount Isa the most important industrial and commercial centre in northwest Queensland.

Below: Coopers Creek, site of the last camp of the ill-fated Burke and Wills expedition. The explorers travelled from Melbourne to the Gulf of Carpentaria in 1860-61, but died of starvation early in the return journey.

Published by National Book Distributors and Publishers
3/2 Aquatic Drive, Frenchs Forest, NSW 2086, Australia

First edition 1982
Second edition 1984
Paperbound edition 1986
Reprinted 1988 (twice), 1993, 1994
© Geoff Higgins and National Book Distributors and
   Publishers

Typeset by Deblaere Typesetting Pty Ltd
Printed in Hong Kong by Everbest Printing Co. Ltd

National Library of Australia Card numbers and
ISBN 1-86302-289-9

# QUEENSLAND

Below: The border of Queensland and the Northern Territory on the rarely used Gulf Road.

Below right: This converted London bus began its run on the Normanton to Croydon railway in the 1930s, and is still in operation.

Bottom: The railway station at Normanton.

Above: Normanton, once a thriving gold town, now has a population of only eight hundred.

Above right: The Millaa Millaa Falls in north Queensland.

Below: Smoke from bushfires almost engulfs a road train on its way through the Gulf country.

Below right: The Daintree River, north Queensland.

Right: The Millstream Falls, the widest in Australia, receive their water from the Atherton Tableland.

Cook's Pillar at Cooktown, where Captain Cook beached in 1770 to repair damage when the *Endeavour* ran aground on the Great Barrier Reef.

Left: Cairns entices both young and old with its relaxed yet colourful atmosphere. Mainly dependent on sugar for its wealth, it is also a haven for deep-sea anglers from September to December when black marlin and other gamefish frequent the coastal waters.

Right: Lake Eacham, a crater lake more than seven hundred metres above sea level in the Atherton Tableland.

The Barron Gorge, Atherton Tableland.

Below: Sooty terns at the Michaelmas Cay breeding sanctuary, off the coast near Cairns.

A typical north Queensland house, with magnificent wide verandahs.

Left: A north Queensland rodeo, popular with spectators and participants alike.

Below: A festive night in Townsville.

An old goldmine at Ravenswood.

Ravenswood is now almost a ghost town after its brief life as a goldmining centre.

Above left: Bowen is famous for its mangoes, but it also has beautiful beaches.

Below left: Castle Hill stands sentinel over Townsville, a blossoming city growing rich on metallic ores, beef and wool from the west, and sugar and timber from the coastal region.

Right: The underwater observatory at Hook Island, where the coral reef can also be seen from glass-bottomed boats.

Above: A giant turtle on the Great Barrier Reef.

A dry creek bed in outback Queensland.

Poolside relaxation at Daydream Island.

Top: Daydream Island, one of the more lavish resorts in the Whitsunday group, has lush tropical vegetation.

Centre: Sailing at South Molle Island.

Bottom: Lorikeets on South Molle Island.

36

Above left: South Molle Island, in the middle of the Whitsunday Passage. This hilly island is clothed in grassland or rainforest, and has several superb beaches.

Left: Shute Harbour is the gateway to more than a hundred tropical islands in the beautiful Whitsunday Passage.

Airlie Beach, northeast of Proserpine.

Top left: Sunset at Cannonvale.

Centre left: Low tide at Vines Creek, Mackay.

Left: Salt flats near Bajool on the Fitzroy River delta.

Mackay produces one-third of Australia's tonnage in sugar. An attractive and progressive city, it contains many fine examples of Victorian, Edwardian and 'Queensland-style' architecture.

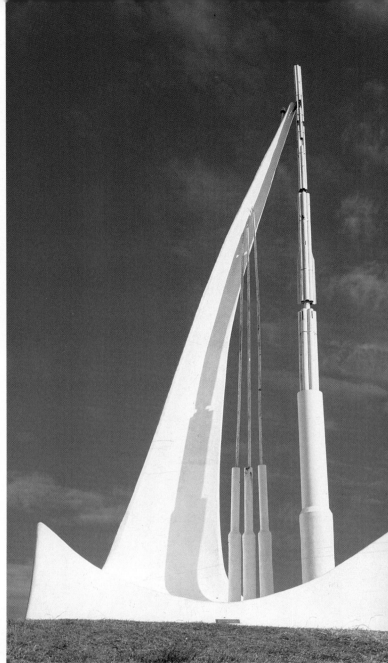

The 'singing ship' memorial to Captain Cook at Emu Park, overlooking Keppel Bay, contains hidden organ pipes that create musical sounds whenever the wind blows.

Top left: A beach at Emu Park.

Centre left: Brahmin cattle are a common sight in northern Queensland.

Above right: Rockhampton's Customs House, built in 1901, is one of the architectural masterpieces of Queensland.

Left and right: Rockhampton, a booming regional centre, is supported by pastoral and mining industries. Magnificent Victorian buildings testify to the aspirations of its founders.

The harbour at Gladstone.

Below left: A typical Queensland house at Gladstone.

Below: A storm approaches Gladstone's harbour.

Above right: Heron Island, a coral cay on the Great Barrier Reef, is a resting place for terns, gulls, muttonbirds and turtles, while its accessible reef is inhabited by more than a thousand varieties of fish and two hundred varieties of coral.

Right and far right: The largest sand island in the world, Fraser Island is rich in mineral deposits and timber.

The lighthouse at Double Island Point.

Left: A giant fig tree at Maryborough.

Far left: Exploring for coral on
Lady Elliott Island.

Coolum Beach, south of
Noosa.

Far right: A view
of Tewantin's 'Big Shell'.

Right: The 'House of
Bottles' at Tewantin.

The wreck of the *Cherry Venture* on Teewah Beach, north of Noosa.

Top: coloured sand display at the 'Big Shell' at Tewantin, in Cooloola National Park.

Centre: The Sunshine Coast is the near north coast's answer to the Gold Coast south of Brisbane. This view includes the Maroochydore airstrip and the Surfair Hotel.

Bottom: Grass-skiing is rapidly becoming a popular sport at Nambour.

47

Peregian Beach, on the way to Noosa, is a favourite with surfers.

Right: A homestead at the Glasshouse Mountains, on the Bruce Highway near Beerwah. The mountains were named in 1770 by Captain Cook.

Centre far left: At the Sun Coast Dairy, near Nambour, the 'Big Cow' houses audio-visual displays on the dairy industry.

Centre left: Australia's largest macadamia nut factory is next door to the Sunshine Plantation, near Nambour. Macadamias, also known as Queensland bush nuts, have become a major industry in Hawaii since they were introduced there from Queensland.

Bottom left: Sorting pine-apples for the Golden Circle Cannery at Nambour.

Bottom far left: The sixteen-metre-high 'Big Pineapple' at the Sunshine Plantation, seven kilometres south of Nambour, includes an observation deck on the top floor.

Below right: A model of a reptile at Tanawha, a hundred kilometres north of Brisbane.

Below far right: The Storey Bridge, one of several crossing the Brisbane River.

Left: Sprawling, sub-tropical Brisbane is Australia's third largest city.

Below left: Queensland's Parliament House, opened in 1869, was designed by Charles Tiffin in a 'tropical Renaissance' style.

Below: A famous Brisbane landmark, 'The Old Windmill' was built by forced labour in 1829 and is one of the few buildings remaining from Queensland's convict era.

Right: Major Mitchell cockatoo.

Far right: A pelican in its natural habitat.

Left: Among the attractions of the Botanic Gardens at Mount Cootha is the Geo-Dome, which houses many varieties of tropical plants.

Below: Brisbane's City Hall dominates King George Square.

Above: The Brisbane River.

Below: Government House, set in magnificent tropical gardens at Bardon.

52

Above: A game of 'Big Chess' is one of the many attractions of Cavill Avenue in Surfers Paradise.

Top centre: The Nerang River at Southport is a popular venue for watersport enthusiasts.

Top right: Fishing is a popular sport along the Gold Coast.

There are regular competitions between the many surf lifesaving clubs along the Gold Coast.

Below right: Tourism has long been Surfers' year-round money spinner.

Below: Currumbin Bird Sanctuary, founded in 1947, is now administered by the National Trust.

Surfers Paradise, 'capital' of the Gold Coast.

Above: Australia-wide, it's known as 'Surfers' — paradise is taken for granted.

Left: Coolangatta, southernmost point of Queensland's Miami-like Gold Coast.

54

Tropical rainforest at Mount Tamborine.

# NEW SOUTH WALES

Right: Opal mining at Lightning Ridge. The fields attract gem fossickers from all over Australia, the chief attraction being the valuable black opal which is found only here.

Below: The Bluff, Tenterfield.

Far right: Tropical ferns and blackboys at the Gibraltar Range near Glen Innes.

Below right: Morning mist at Gibraltar Range National Park near Glen Innes.

Top far left: Glen Innes Public School, built of sandstone and dating from the Victorian era.

Centre far left: The tower clock and Weiley's Hotel at Grafton which is famous for its jacaranda trees and the annual Jacaranda Festival.

Bottom far left: The 'Capital of the Banana Coast', Coffs Harbour is a popular coastal resort roughly halfway between Sydney and Brisbane.

Above: Booloominbah Mansion, administration centre for the University of New England, Armidale.

Above left: The 'Big Banana' at Coffs Harbour leaves no doubt about the area's main agricultural crop.

Left: A banana plantation at Coffs Harbour.

Above: Tamworth, an attractive and prosperous city in the Peel Valley at the foot of the Wentworth Mountains, is the centre of a rich rural area. Self-styled 'capital' of New England, Tamworth is also the nation's country music capital.

Left: The Warrumbungle Ranges, with their deep gorges and precipitous rock faces, are a paradise for mountaineers and bushwalkers. Warrumbungle National Park contains some spectacular mountain scenery.

Above left: 'The Breadknife', a ninety-metre-high sliver of rock in the Warrumbungle Ranges.

Right: Fantasy Glades at Port Macquarie.

Above right: Trial Bay, near Kempsey, was named after *The Trial*, a brig stolen from Sydney by convicts and wrecked here in 1816. The town's gaol, first used in 1886, has been partially restored and houses a museum and a kiosk.

The Pacific Highway, the main coastal route linking Sydney and Brisbane, crosses the Manning River just outside of Taree.

Left: Trees such as the *Angophora* and the paperbark rank high on the list of Myall Lakes' treasures. The white-boled paperbarks bordering the lakes and swamps are especially beautiful.

Below left: Stockton Bridge, Newcastle.

Above: Lovers of hand-painted wooden toys head for Sugar Creek Road, Smith's Lakes, where a family business thrives on this revived craft.

Above: Myall Lakes
National Park. A spectacular
headland, long expanses of
beach, superb rainforests
and ten thousand hectares of
lakes are among the Park's
many attractions.

Right: The yacht club at
Belmont.

Above left: Surfing — and
its associated highly trained
rescue teams — is as much a
part of life in Newcastle as in
other Australian coastal
areas.

Left: Nobbys, at the
entrance to Newcastle
Harbour, was formerly an
island and a solitary con-
finement women's prison in
convict times. It is now
linked to the mainland by a
breakwater.

Left: Sydney has long been acclaimed as one of the more beautiful of the world's harbour cities, with its famed Harbour Bridge, Opera House and Circular Quay.

Right: From Dawes Point, the Bridge lunges north across the harbour. Under the shadow of its approaches, in a small area known simply as The Rocks, are some of Sydney's oldest buildings.

Below: This hundred-year-old post box was designed for the convenience of riders on horseback, but remains in use today.

Below right: The heart of 'downtown' Sydney is Martin Place. Once busy with vehicular traffic, it is now a pedestrian mall.

65

Top: Harbour views from Sydney's Taronga Park Zoo.

Above: The fountain in Australia Square.

Right: Fiftieth anniversary celebrations for the Bridge.

Top left: The city skyline, looking across Farm Cove from the Botanical Gardens.

Above left: Buskers have become a familiar sight in Sydney.

Top: Hyde Park is a major venue for events celebrating the Festival of Sydney each January.

Above: Paddy's Market, synonymous with fresh fruit and vegetables for more than a century.

Left: Sydney's Hyde Park is by far the largest park in the inner city area. St Mary's Cathedral, in the background, is the seat of the Roman Catholic primate.

Left: Hyde Park — an oasis of calm in a pulsating city.

Above: Brooklyn, on the Hawkesbury River, is a popular starting point for fishing and boating enthusiasts.

Above: The reserve at Long Neck Lagoon, near Cattai on the Wiseman's Ferry Road.

Below: All that remains of the MacDonald Valley Inn, near Wiseman's Ferry.

Bottom: The Nepean River at Penrith.

Above: Golden Gully, Hill End. The huge Beyers and Holtermann nugget was found near here in 1872.

Top left: The remains of the shale oil plant at Newnes in the Wolgan Valley.

Above left: Bowral, a popular resort area, is the scene of a tulip festival in October.

Right and far right: Bushell's Lagoon, at Wilberforce on the Hawkesbury River, during a drought that dried it out for only the second time in recorded history.

Left: The Kanangra Walls in the Blue Mountains are just one of many spectacular sights in this popular resort area. On a clear day the Bridge can be seen from here — though it's more than a hundred kilometres away!

Left: Echo Point lookout at Katoomba, in the Blue Mountains. Outstanding rock formations in this area, such as 'The Three Sisters', are floodlit at night.

Below far left: Blue Gum Forest in the Blue Mountains.

Below left: Autumn in Mount Wilson, one of the Blue Mountains' historic towns.

Above: 'Caves House' at Jenolan Caves. Jenolan is justly famous for its spectacular limestone caverns.

Above right: Wollemi National Park.

Right: The Colo River, Wollemi National Park.

A boiler once used on the Hill End goldfields.

Left: The Macquarie River, which rises on the west of the Great Dividing Range and services such major towns as Bathurst, Wellington and Dubbo.

Below: The old hospital at Hill End. The township itself is one of the best preserved reminders of the gold rush that took place here a little more than a century ago.

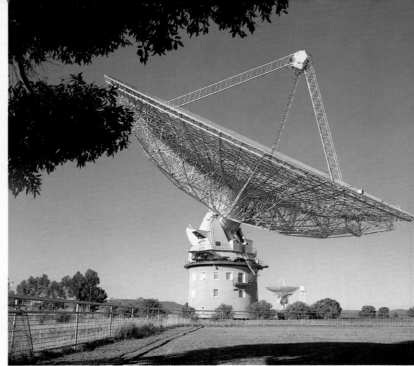

The Lachlan River at Condobolin.

Right: The Silverton gaol and historical museum. The discovery of silver gave Silverton a population of three thousand in 1885, but its mine closed in 1889 and it is now a ghost town.

Above right: The radio telescope at Parkes used by the Radio Physics Department of the CSIRO (Commonwealth Scientific & Industrial Research Organisation) began operating in 1961.

The headquarters of Flying Doctor Service. This service has brought medical aid to outback families for sixty years.

Left: The Darling River at Menindee.

Mungo National Park is noted for its dry lake basins and dunes.

Main picture: An outback road near Ivanhoe.

Above: The copper dome of the Academy of Science, Canberra.

Above left: Outback sunset at Coonamble.

Above right: The Australian Capital Territory embraces grazing land that was originally part of New South Wales. Blundell's Farmhouse is one of the few old homesteads still remaining.

Right: Black Mountain tower, Canberra's main communications centre.

Far left: Anzac Parade, with Parliament House on the left.

Left: The High Court, Canberra. There have been many additions to the city's skyline since the Federal Parliament first sat here in 1927.

The National Library of Australia, Canberra.

Right: Majestic gumtrees at Wee Jasper.

Far right: Yarrangobilly, in the Mount Kosciusko National Park.

Below right: A homestead along the Snowy Mountains Highway.

Below: The Thai Embassy, Canberra. Many embassy buildings in the capital have been modelled on designs indigenous to the countries represented.

Below left: Cockington Green, Canberra.

Above: Thredbo, another ski resort in the Crackenback Range, is only a hundred kilometres from Cooma.

Below: Perisher Valley, a popular ski resort in the Snowy Mountains during the winter season. At other times of the year the area is a favourite with anglers, bushwalkers and boating enthusiasts.

Below: The Snowy Mountains Highway near Tumut.

Perisher Valley.

Below right: Frozen fantasy, at Perisher.

Below: Mount Kosciusko National Park. The mountain, the highest in Australia at 2230 metres, was first explored in 1840 by the Polish explorer Paul Strzelecki.

Lake Jindabyne, in the Snowy Mountains, is well stocked with trout, and is also ideal for boating and water-skiing.

Left: A storm approaches in the Snowy Mountains.

Right: Pastoral scene near Cooma.

84

Along the southern coast of New South Wales.

Inset: A south-coast seascape.

A waterfall in Kanangra-Boyd National Park, south of Jenolan Caves in the Blue Mountains.

Above right: Li-loing, a water activity which is increasing in popularity.

Right: The Pinnacles, in Ben Boyd National Park.

Fishing boats at Jervis Bay. In 1915 jurisdiction of this fine natural port was transferred from New South Wales to the Australian Capital Territory, to give the Federal Capital sea access.

Above right: This former hotel at Culcairn, built in 1860, is now known as the Woolpack Inn Museum. Its exhibits include the complete plant of an old cordial factory, a bakery, farm equipment and horse-drawn vehicles.

Right: Twelve kilometres east of Albury is the Hume Weir, part of the immense Murray River irrigation system.

Morgan's Hill Lookout at Walla Walla, eighteen kilometres from
Culcairn.

# VICTORIA

The birthplace of Captain James Cook, this tiny cottage was brought from Yorkshire and re-erected in Melbourne in 1934.

St Paul's Cathedral in Swanston Street.

Left: The Shrine of Remembrance, on Melbourne's St Kilda Road.

Below: Prince's Bridge, one of several crossing the Yarra River.
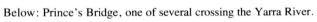

95

Above left: The imposing Flinders Street Station has visually dominated this area since its opening in 1910.

Above far left: Collins Street, home to many elegant restaurants and fashionable boutiques, is Melbourne's answer to Paris's Rue de la Paix or Rome's Via Condotti.

Above: The heavily forested Dandenong Ranges are only 50 kilometres from Melbourne.

Left: The Royal Botanic Gardens on Domain Road.

Right: Although Sydney-siders hate to admit it, Melbourne was Australia's financial capital for many years. As well as many imposing city buildings, its wealth in the late Victorian era gave birth to many public buildings such as this.

97

Natural beauty — in this case a young tree-fern — in the Dandenong Ranges.

Below: A stretch of the Great Ocean Road, which covers three hundred kilometres of magnificent scenery from Torquay to Peterborough.

Right: The 'Twelve Apostles', Port Campbell National Park.

Above: Another of Port Campbell National Park's natural attractions.

Above left: Sunset at Port Campbell National Park which is notable for its spectacular rock formations.

A grotto in Port Campbell National Park.

...etrified forest at Cape
...ridgewater, near Port-
...and.

...ight: A boatshed on
...e Hopkins River at
...arrnambool, a popular
...oastal resort.

Mildura, on the Murray River, was once a busy inland port with more than a hundred vessels calling in a six-month season. In recent years, restored paddle-steamers serving the tourist trade have become a major attraction.

Right: The Mackenzie Falls in the Grampians.

Below right: PS *Melbourne* departing on a two-hour Murray River cruise.

Facing page: The Grampians, the southwestern extremity of the Great Dividing Range that runs inland of Australia's east coast from Queensland through to Victoria, are a paradise for bushwalkers, rock-climbers and naturalists.

A softwood forest to the west of Wodonga.

Left: Cattle at Swan Hill seek shelter from the midday sun.

Below: Beechworth is one of Victoria's best preserved and most beautiful gold towns. Thirty of its public buildings have been classified as historically important by the National Trust.

Ned Kelly was once held in this sandstone goal at Beechworth.

The old Chinese cemetery at Beechworth.

Left: Waterfall at Beechworth.

Right: The Ovens River at Porepunkah, majestically set at the foot of Mount Buffalo National Park.

106

Early settlers planted many imported deciduous trees in and around Bright, which holds an annual 'Festival of Falling Leaves'.

Below: Bright, an old mining town in the foothills of the Victorian Alps. Remains of diggings on the alluvial goldfields can still be seen.

Right: Mount Beauty, near Falls Creek in the Victorian Alps.

Below right: Ice stalactites at Mount Hotham in the Victorian Alps.

Above: Winter at Mount Buffalo.

Right: A quaint church in the historic town of Tarraville.

Top left: Alpine flowers greet springtime at Mount Buffalo.

Bottom left: 'Buffalo House', a popular spot for ski enthusiasts at Mount Buffalo.

Centre left: Mount Buffalo's facilities for downhill and cross- country skiing attract thousands of skiers during the season.

Above left: Mount Hiawatha, near Yarram.

Above: The harbour at Port Albert. One of Victoria's earliest settlements, Port Albert was established as a port before Melbourne. In the 1850s, thousands of hopeful miners arrived here on their way to the newly discovered goldfields.

Left: Wilson's Promontory, at the southernmost tip of the Australian mainland, is one of Victoria's largest and most spectacular national parks.

Right: Tidal river in Wilson's Promontory National Park.

Above right: This whale-shaped rock is in Wilson's Promontory National Park.

Above far right: Lake Surprise lies in the crater of an extinct volcano at Mount Eccles.

Pyramid Island, near Phillip Island at the entrance to Port Phillip Bay.

Left: The Nobbies, on the southwest side of Phillip Island.

114

# TASMANIA

Below: The coastline of the Tasman Peninsula.

Bottom: Australia's oldest bridge, which crosses the Coal River at Richmond, was built by convicts between 1823 and 1825.

Hobart, Tasmania's capital, is an enchanting harbour-side city at the foot of Mount Wellington.

Left: City Hall, Hobart.

116

Above right: The Royal
Botanic Gardens in the
Queen's Domain.

Right: Government House
stands in the Queen's Domain.

Above left: The convict-built church at Port Arthur which was the most dreaded of early Australia's penal settlement.

Above: Cradle Mountain.

Left: Lake Pedder, created during the first stage of the Gordon River Power Development scheme, is well stocked with trout.

Above: Cradle Mountain — Lake St Clair National Park. Cradle Mountain's fine bushwalks include the eighty-five-kilometre overland track.

Below: Devonport, terminal for the vehicular ferry from Melbourne, derives its wealth from agriculture and food processing.

One of the many beautiful bushwalks on Cradle Mountain.

Below: Russell Falls, at Mount Field, were discovered in 1856.

Mining has been continuous at Queenstown since the discovery of gold here in 1888. This town has been the mining centre of one of the world's richest copper lodes. Over the years fumes from the copper smelter have destroyed much of the vegetation in the immediate area.

Below: Queenstown.

The red granite ranges of The Hazards in the Coles Bay area.

Left: The port of Strahan, in Macquarie Harbour, is the only town on Tasmania's forbidding west coast. Originally a timber-milling town, its growth was boosted by the copper boom at Mount Lyell mine. It now serves as a port for Queenstown, and also supports a small fishing industry.

Below: Lake St Clair, the most beautiful in Tasmania.

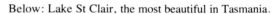

Left: Crayfish can be caught at the fishing port of Bicheno, less than two hundred kilometres from Hobart.

Below left: The vehicular ferry returns to Kettering from Bruny Island, where Captain Cook landed in 1770.

Frenchman's Cap National Park.

Left: St Columba Falls, near Pyengana.

Right: Near St Columba Falls.

Far right: Mount Field National Park.

Above: St Helen's, on George's Bay, is renowned for its crayfish and flounder.

Above right: The Plenty Salmon Ponds, the first successful trout hatchery in Australia, is eleven kilometres west of New Norfolk.

Right: The 'Tessellated Pavement' at Eaglehawk, a narrow isthmus separating the Tasman Sea from the Forester Peninsula.

Left: The Derwent River near New Norfolk.

Left: The Ross Bridge is a monument to the skill of convict craftsmen.

Below left: Scotts Peak Dam in southwest Tasmania.

Launceston, Tasmania's second largest city, was founded in 1824.

Below: The Penny Royal Water Mill Complex was originally situated at Barton, but was later moved stone by stone to Launceston.

Below right: Millers Tavern in the Penny Royal Water Mill complex at Launceston.

JOLLY MILLER

THE MILLERS TAVERN BAR

Cataract Gorge is a few minutes' drive from Launceston. The gorge can be crossed by a suspension bridge or a scenic chairlift.

Left: Pastureland at Pyengana.

# SOUTH AUSTRALIA

The Mount Lofty Ranges, near Adelaide.

The spacious and well-planned city of Adelaide, its central area completely surrounded by parklands, is set on a narrow coastal plain between the Mount Lofty Ranges and St Vincent's Gulf.

Above right: Major events at the Adelaide Arts Festival take place in the magnificent festival centre complex on the banks of the Torrens River.

Right: A view from Adelaide's festival centre.

Far right: Rundle Mall, a busy shopping complex in the heart of Adelaide.

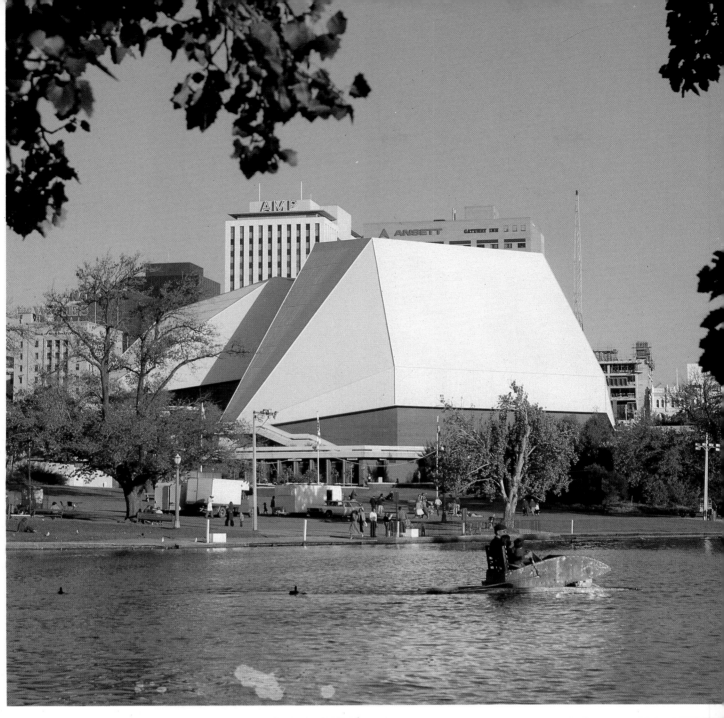

North Adelaide has a good share of fine colonial buildings, including old hotels with wrought-iron 'lace', stone cottages and stately houses.

Right: An example of the buildings of the Victorian era to be seen in North Adelaide.

Below left: Seppeltsfield, one of the major wineries in the Barossa Valley. The valley was so named by German immigrants who settled the area in the last century. The Barossa Valley produces about a quarter of Australia's wines.

Below far right: *The Murray River Queen* evokes memories of the golden riverboat days.

Below right: Writing about the Murray River in 1830, Charles Sturt said, 'The banks of the channel with the trees and the rocks were reflected in the tranquil waters whose surface was unruffled save by the thousands of wild fowl that rose before us . . .'

Left: The vineyards at Clare
were established in 1848 by two
Jesuit priests from Austria,
and continue to produce prize-
winning wines.

Far left: Alligator Gorge in the
Mount Remarkable National
Park, near Wilmington.

Below: Deserted hotel at
Hawker, in the Flinders Ranges.

The vast natural amphitheatre of Wilpena Pound, in the Flinders Ranges, is one of Australia's more extraordinary geological formations.

Above right: Kanyakka, one of many properties abandoned in the 1890s with the failure of the wheat crops.

Right: Brachina Gorge, north of Wilpena in the Flinders Ranges.

Warren Gorge, a popular climbing area near Quorn in the Flinders Ranges.

Top: The stony Flinders Ranges are normally dry; here the land is rippled with creeks after heavy rainfall.

Left: Chambers Gorge, in the northern part of the Flinders Ranges, is easily accessible by vehicle or on foot.

139

Mount Billy Creek at Wilkawillana Gorge in the Flinders Ranges.

Below: The Aroona Valley, with the peaks of the Wilpena Ranges in the background.

Below left: All that remains of once-thriving Aroona Homestead in the Aroona Valley.

Near Wilpena Pound in the Flinders Ranges.

Right: Wildlife is abundant in the Flinders Ranges.

Far right: The Flinders Ranges are part of a mountain chain extending almost eight hundred kilometres from St Vincent's Gulf. The most spectacular areas of the ranges lie to the northeast of Port Augusta and north of Hawker.

141

Sheep graze at Wilpena Pound.

Right: Outback sunset.

Below right: On the road to Blinman.

Below: Bunyaroo Valley, north of Wilpena in the Flinders Ranges.

A dry salt pan on the road between William Creek and Lake Eyre.

Right: Lake Eyre.

Below left: By all means put a letter in the 'mail box' — but don't expect it to be delivered!

Below right: The Aboriginal name for Coober Pedy, almost a thousand kilometres from Adelaide in the heart of the outback, is 'white fellows' hole in the ground' — appropriate enough, for only by living in underground homes can the inhabitants endure the searing heat (often above 54°C) of summer and the numbing cold of a desert winter. Opals were discovered here in 1911, and today there are hundreds of mines in the area.

Bottom: In 1974, Lake Eyre was filled with water for only the second time since Europeans had explored the desert. Now, after years without substantial rain, it is almost dry again.

The entrance to a Coober Pedy 'dugout'.

Above right: Opal-mining is a multi-million dollar industry in South Australia's outback.

Above centre: 'Noodling' for opal in the waste from the shafts which pit the area.

Above far right: Paddy melons in the South Australian outback.

Right: The dingo proof fence near Marree.

Left: A 'dugout' home at Coober Pedy.

# WESTERN AUSTRALIA

Although a bitumen highway has recently replaced the old
corrugated, gravel road across the Nullarbor Plain from Adelaide
into Western Australia, the country traversed in this enormously
long drive remains hot, inhospitable and almost devoid of
any settlement.

Cape Le Grand National Park, east of Esperance, includes a spectacular coastline with many attractive beaches.

Right: Once a vital link in Australia's east-west communications, the old telegraph station at Eucla was abandoned when the telegraph line was closed down in 1927.

Below right: Coastal dunes at Eucla.

Lucky Bay, in Cape Le Grand National Park.

Left: 'Natural Bridge' at Albany.

Right: Sunset over King George Sound, near Albany which is Western Australia's oldest town.

Below right: A full-scale replica of the brig *Amity* which brought Major Lockyer and a party of convicts to found the settlement of Albany in 1826.

Below far right: Fifteen-metre-high 'Wave Rock', at Hyden, is estimated to be 2700 million years old.

151

The town of Pemberton is surrounded by forests of karri, one of the world's tallest hardwood trees.

Above left: Prevailing westerly winds make Australia's southwest corner one of the wettest areas on the continent.

Left: Eighty kilometres north of Albany is the Stirling Range National Park, a favourite spot for bushwalkers and — in springtime — wildflower enthusiasts.

Right: Cossack, now a ghost town on the coast.

Beedelup National Park, near Pemberton.

Below: Easy going Perth, the capital of Western Australia. The people are friendly, the beaches beautiful and the climate near perfect. Perth is Australia's sunniest capital, with an average of 7.8 hours of sunshine a day.

Right: 'Woodbridge', a historic riverside house at Guildford, near Perth. Built in 1885, it is now run by the National Trust.

Below right: The Maritime Museum and Art Centre in Fremantle.

Perth's old court house, built in the 1830s, has also served as a theatre, concert hall and church.

Above right: The Round House at Fremantle, built in 1829, is the oldest building in Western Australia.

Right: The Pinnacle Desert's unusual rock formations are in Nambung National Park, two hundred kilometres north of Perth.

Left: St. George's Terrace, Perth.

Below: Hay Street Mall, Perth.

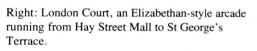

Above: The Dutch navigator Willem de Vlamingh named Rottnest Island after mistaking the quokka, a species of wallaby, for a large rat.

Right: London Court, an Elizabethan-style arcade running from Hay Street Mall to St George's Terrace.

The Pinnacle Desert.

Left: Greenough, on the coast road twenty-four kilometres south of Geraldton, is an historic small town with museums and relics of buildings such as this old flour mill.

Far left: Prevailing winds tell tales.

Kalbarri National Park.

Below: The Murchison River in Kalbarri National Park, located 661 kilometres north of Perth between Geraldton and Carnarvon.

The Hutt River 'Province' has claimed independence from the Commonwealth of Australia and from the state of Western Australia. Its residents refuse to pay state or federal taxation, and have their own 'government', postage stamps and economic policies.

The Overseas Telecommunications Commission earth station and Radio Australia base are both located at Brown's Range near Carnarvon. The OTC station's mammoth reflector (known as 'the big dish') measures 29 metres in diameter.

Below: The Wittenoom Gorge.

Mount Tom Price, the 'Mountain of Iron'.

Below: Mining for iron at Mount Tom Price.

161

The waters of the Fortescue and other rivers have carved spectacular gorges.

Above right: Chichester Range National Park.

Right: Clear pools beneath the Fortescue Falls.

Above: Aircraft control tower at Port Hedland.

Above left: The branch library at Roeburne, not far from Port Hedland.

Left: Salt-mining is an important local industry as Port Hedland. Established on a narrow island linked to the mainland by three long causeways, the Port is the fastest-growing town in the state. Enormous tonnages of iron ore are carried from here to other Australian ports and world markets.

In the early years of this
century, Broome was a
boomtown supported by the
lucrative pearl-fishing trade;
today it is a quiet, scattered
settlement of only three
thousand people.

Right: Cultured pearls spelt
doom for the pearl-fishing
industry. Now only a few
luggers continue the search
for pearl oysters.

Far right: Broome Court
House, built in 1888, originally housed transmitting
equipment for the submarine
telegraph line linking
Broome to Java.

Above left: Windjana Gorge on the Fitzroy River, Kimberley.

Left: Tunnel Creek, Kimberley.

Geikie Gorge, near Fitzroy Crossing in the Kimberley region. Large permanent waterholes are home to sharks, sawfish and freshwater crocodiles.

Above far left: Ivanhoe Crossing at Kununurra.

Above left: The old police station at Kimberley.

Left: Kununurra (an Aboriginal word for 'big water') lies at the heart of the Ord River Scheme in the far north of the east Kimberley region.

Above: Lake Argyle, the largest man-made lake in Australia, holds nine times the volume of the water in Sydney Harbour.

Dead Horse Gap, Lake Argyle

Left: Lake Argyle was formed by the building of the Ord River Dam, which was completed in 1972.

# NORTHERN TERRITORY

Oberi Rock in Arnhem Land, east of Darwin. The Arnhem Land
Aboriginal Reserve, covering eight million hectares, is outstanding
among Australia's wilderness areas.

Above: Aboriginal art on Nourlangie Rock in the Kakadu National Park.

Above left: Aboriginal children in Arnhem Land.

Left: The East Alligator River crossing at the entrance to the Arnhem Land Aboriginal Reserve.

Rock-hard mounds of digested mud, built by termites, are a feature of the 'top end' of the Northern Territory.

Below: Yellow Water Lagoon, at Jim Jim in the Kakadu National Park.

The 'Old Vic' pub, recently restored and diversified, has been a favourite Darwin watering hole for many years.

The Law Courts in Darwin.

Left: Douglas Hot Springs on the Douglas River, a few kilometres from Pine Creek.

Below: The residence of the Northern Territory Administrator, built in 1870, is one of the few Darwin buildings to have survived the ravages of World War II bombing and the devastation wrought by Cyclone Tracey at the end of 1974.

Above far left: Festival time in Darwin.

Above left: Aboriginal dancers in Darwin.

Left: Vestey Beach at Fanny Bay, where Ross and Keith Smith landed their Vickers Vimy aircraft in 1919, thus completing the first flight from the United Kingdom to Australia.

Above: In Katherine Gorge National Park the river flows between towering brilliantly coloured walls.

Pandanus palms along the Katherine River which was discovered by John McDouall Stuart in 1862 and named after the daughter of one of his expedition's sponsors.

Right: 'The Devil's Marbles', ten kilometres south of Tennant Creek. According to Aboriginal legend, these huge boulders are eggs laid by the mythical Rainbow Snake.

Below: Twenty-six kilometres from Tennant Creek is this memorial to Flynn of the Inland, pioneer of Australia's Flying Doctor Service.

Above: The Overland Telegraph Station, three kilometres outside of Alice Springs. The overland telegraph, completed in 1872, linked Port Augusta with Darwin, from where the telegraph was carried by submarine cable to Java. The station's (and its township's) buildings have been restored to the style of the period.

Top: Hermannsburg Mission, north of Palm Valley.

Palm Valley in the Finke Gorge National Park, a twelve-hour drive
from Alice Springs. The Finke River is said to be one of the world's
oldest water courses.

Ghost gums in the Ormiston Gorge.

Below: Wild donkeys are found in many areas of Central Australia.

Right: Ross River, eighty-five kilometres east of Alice Springs.

Below right: Gosses Bluff, in the MacDonnell Ranges.

'The Lost City', on private property in King's Canyon, is 330 kilometres southwest of Alice Springs.

Left: Glen Helen Gorge, on the west of the MacDonnell Ranges at Finke River.

Chambers Pillar, in Central Australia, was named in 1860 by the explorer John McDouall Stuart in honour of his expedition's patron.

Below: King's Canyon.

Ghost gums in the MacDonnell Ranges.

Left: The monument to Albert Namatjira at Hermannsburg Mission. Namatjira became world famous in the 1950s as the first Aboriginal to paint Australian landscapes in a European style.

Facing page, top three pictures: Nine kilometres in circumference, and rising 348 metres above the surrounding desert, Ayers Rock is the world's largest monolith and one of its great natural wonders. Caves undercut in the base of the rock have been decorated by Aborigines, for whom it is a sacred dreaming place.

Right: The 'Bell Cave' at Ayers Rock.

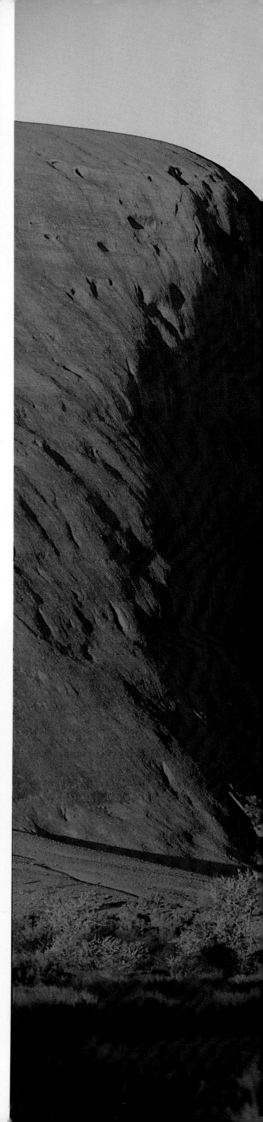

The dingo or native dog.

This five-hundred-metre-high monolith is one of twenty-eight comprising the Olgas, not far from Ayers Rock.

Camels now roam free in central Australia.

Four wheel drives are a popular mode of transport in the Australian Outback.

# Index

Adelaide 132, 134
Airlie Beach 37
Albany 150
Alice Springs 180, 182, 184
Alligator Gorge 136
Armidale 59
Arnhem Land 171, 172
Aroona Valley 140
Australian Capital Territory 79, 80
Ayers Rock 186, 188

Bajool 39
Bardon 52
Barossa Valley 134
Barron Gorge 26
Barton 129
Beechworth 104, 106
Beedelup National Park 154
Belmont 63
Ben Boyd National Park 88
Bicheno 125
Blinman 142
Blue Mountains 71, 73, 89
Bowen 31
Bowral 71
Brachina Gorge 137
Bright 108
Brisbane 50
Brisbane River 52
Brooklyn 69
Brooms Range 160
Bruny Island 125
Bunyaroo Valley 142
Bushell's Lagoon 71

Cairns 24
Canberra 79, 80
Cannonvale 39
Cape Bridgewater 101
Cape Le Grand National Park 149, 150
Carnarvon 12, 159, 160
Castle Hill 31
Castlereagh River 115
Cataract Gorge 130
Cattai 70
Chambers Gorge 139
Chambers Pillar 185
Chichester Range National Park 163
Clare 136
Coal River 115
Coffs Harbour 59
Coles Bay 123
Colo River 73
Condobolin 75
Coober Pedy 144, 145, 146
Cook's Pillar 24
Cooktown 24
Coolangatta 54
Coolum Beach 45
Cooma 84
Coonamble 79
Coopers Creek 20
Cossack 153
Crackenback Range 82
Cradle Mountain 119, 120, 121
Culcairn 90
Currumbin 53

Daintree River 22
Dandenong Ranges 97, 98
Darling River 76
Darwin 175, 176
Dawes Point 65
Daydream Island 35
Derwent River 127
Devonport 120
Double Island Point 44
Douglas River 175

Eaglehawk 127
East Alligator River 172
Echo Point 73
Emu Park 40
Eucla 149

Falls Creek 108
Fanny Bay 177
Farm Cove 68
Finke Gorge National Park 181
Finke River 181, 184
Fitzroy River, Qld 39
Fitzroy River, WA 167
Flinders Ranges 1, 10, 136, 137, 139, 140, 141, 142
Forester Peninsula 127
Fortescue Falls 162
Fraser Island 42
Fremantle 154, 156
Frenchman's Cap National Park 125

Geikie Gorge 167
George's Bay 127
Geraldton 158, 159
Gibraltar Range 56
Gladstone 42
Glasshouse Mountains 48
Glen Helen Gorge 184
Glen Innes 56, 59
Gold Coast 53, 54
Golden Gully 71
Grafton 59
Grampians, The 103
Great Barrier Reef 32, 42
Great Dividing Range 103
Greenough 158
Guildford 154

Hawker 136, 141
Hawkesbury River 69, 71
Hazards, The 123
Heron Island 42
Hill End 71, 74
Hobart 116
Hook Island 32
Hopkins River 101
Hutt River 159
Hyden 150

Ivanhoe 77

Jenolan Caves 73, 89
Jervis Bay 90
Jim Jim 173

Kakadu National Park 172, 173
Kalbarri National Park 159
Kanangra-Boyd National Park 88
Kanangra Walls 71
Katherine Gorge National Park 177
Katherine River 178
Katoomba 73
Kettering 125
Kimberley 167, 169
King George Sound 150
King's Canyon 184, 185
Kununurra 169

Lachlan River 75
Lady Elliott Island 44
Lake Argyle 169, 170
Lake Eacham 26
Lake Eyre 145
Lake Jindabyne 84
Lake Pedder 119
Lake St Clair 123
Lake St Clair National Park 120
Lake Surprise 112
Launceston 129

Lightning Ridge 56
Long Neck Lagoon 70
Lucky Bay 150

MacDonnell Ranges 182, 184, 186
Mackay 39
Mackenzie Falls 103
Macquarie Harbour 123
Manning River 61
Marree 146
Maryborough 44
Maryvale 14
Melbourne 95, 97
Menindee 76
Michaelmas Cay 26
Mildura 103
Millaa Millaa Falls 22
Millstream Falls 24
Mount Beauty 108
Mount Billy Creek 140
Mount Buffalo 111
Mount Buffalo National Park 106
Mount Cootha 51
Mount Eccles 112
Mount Field 121
Mount Field National Park 8, 126
Mount Hiawatha 112
Mount Hotham 108
Mount Isa 20
Mount Kosciusko 80, 83
Mount Lofty Ranges 131, 132
Mount Lyell 123
Mount Remarkable National Park 136
Mount Tamborine 55
Mount Tom Price 161
Mount Wellington 116
Mount Wilson 73
Mungo National Park 77
Murchison River 159
Murray River 103, 135
Myall Lakes 62, 63

Nambour 47, 48
Nambung National Park 156
Nepean River 70
Nerang River 53
New England 59, 60
New Norfolk 127
Newcastle 62, 63
Newnes 71
Nobbies, The 114
Nobbys 63
Noosa 47
Normanton 21, 22
Nullarbor Plain 148

Ormiston Gorge 182
Ovens River 106

Palm Valley 181
Parkes 75
Peel Valley 60
Pemberton 153
Penrith 70
Peregian Beach 48
Perisher Valley 82, 83
Perth 154, 156
Peterborough 98
Phillip Island 114
Pinnacle Desert 156, 158
Pinnacles, The 88
Porepunkah 106
Port Albert 112
Port Arthur 119
Port Augusta 141
Port Campbell 6
Port Campbell National Park 98, 100
Port Hedland 164
Port Macquarie 60

Port Phillip Bay 114
Pyengana 126, 130
Pyramid Island 114

Queen's Domain, the 117
Queenstown 122, 123
Quorn 139

Ravenswood 31
Richmond 115
Rockhampton 40
Rocks, The 65
Roeburne 164
Ross River 182
Rottnest Island 157
Russell Falls 8, 121

St Columba Falls 126
St Helen's 127
St Vincent's Gulf 132, 141
Shute Harbour 2, 37
Silverton 75
Smith's Lakes 62
Snowy Mountains 82, 84
South Molle Island 35, 37
Southport 53
Stirling Range National Park 153
Strahan 123
Sunshine Coast 47
Surfers Paradise 53, 54
Swan Hill 104
Sydney 4, 65, 66

Tamworth 60
Tanawha 48
Taree 61
Tarraville 111
Tasman Peninsula 115
Tasman Sea 127
Teewah Beach 47
Tennant Creek 178
Tenterfield 56
Tewantin 45
Thredbo 82
Torquay 98
Torrens River 132
Townsville 29
Trial Bay 60
Tumut 82
Tunnel Creek 167

Victorian Alps 108
Vines Creek 39

Walla Walla 92
Warren Gorge 139
Warrnambool 101
Warrumbungle Ranges 60
Wee Jasper 80
Wentworth Mountains 60
Whitsunday Passage 37
Wilberforce 71
Wilkawillana Gorge 140
Wilmington 136
Wilpena Pound 137, 140, 141, 142
Wilson's Promontory 112
Wilson's Promontory National Park 112
Windjana Gorge 166
Wiseman's Ferry 70
Wittenoom Gorge 160
Wolgan Valley 71
Wollemi National Park 73

Yarra River 95
Yarrangobilly 80
Yellow Water Lagoon 173

## ACKNOWLEDGEMENTS

The publishers would like to acknowledge the following photographers and government bodies for their contributions.
   Bill Andrews, p. 95, bottom; p. 125; Trevern Dawes, p. 155, below; Les Green, p. 20, bottom; p. 21; p. 23, bottom; p. 43, bottom right; p. 70; centre right; p. 170, below; Premier's Department, South Australia, p. 134, below; p. 136, above right; Queensland Tourist and Travel Corporation, p. 53, top left, centre and bottom left; Peter Solness, p. 20, top; p. 22; p. 23, top; p. 24; p. 25; p. 26; p. 27; p. 28, p. 31, bottom; p. 38, bottom; p. 43, bottom left; p. 50, top left; p. 104, top right and left; p. 135 bottom left and right; p. 136, top left; p. 141, below left; p. 141, top; p. 180, bottom; Tasmanian Department of Tourism, p. 115, bottom; p. 116, top; p. 120; p. 123; p. 124, bottom; p. 126, below; p. 128, top.